# Healing Laughter

## THE DANCE FOR
## BREAST CANCER SURVIVORS

ISBN — 978-0-578-17546-1

PUBLISHER:    *C.L. Smith*
              *Albany, OR 97322*

*Book design by Stacie Marshall, Hill Design Co.*

*Printed in the United States of America*

# Healing Laughter

## THE DANCE FOR
## BREAST CANCER SURVIVORS

By Connielee Smith

I am a survivor. I have looked in the mirror and seen
that I am no longer the woman I remember.
I will never be that woman again. Instead I am better.
My shape and form have been molded by life, and as
such, makes me know that change is just fine.
We all change. I am happier today than all of the
yesterdays combined because I am a survivor walking
this path with you, my family, and friends.

# Contents

# Endorsements

"I found *Healing Laughter* to be a very unique and encouraging book written to those going through cancer or difficult and serious struggles in life. This book will affect the way we walk through difficult times. I would highly recommend this book."

— *Connie Ayers*

"Connielee has written an uplifting book explaining the healing qualities of laughter and the importance of inviting joy into your life. There were so many laugh-out-loud moments, this book is a gem!"

— *Jeanna Billings, Founder, Shaman's Spirit*

"This book was wonderful! It brought back memories of my own diagnosis, treatment and reconstruction. I had bi-lateral reconstruction after my first bout with breast cancer and then had a recurrence. My implants had ruptured anyway prior to my diagnosis so I had trans-flap bi-lateral reconstruction a second time. I always laugh about being on "breasts 5 and 6" when I see a new medical professional and must go over my medical history. Connie's good humored but informative narrative about her own experiences made me feel better about myself as a survivor. I recognized some of her anecdotes but some of her tales brought new understanding of myself. I would recommend this book to those women going through the experience, survivors and anyone who cares about them. Please read it, digest it and use it to make life, not just easier, but more joyful. Find the joy and laughter in your life as Connielee Smith has done in hers."

— *Claudia Perry-St. Andre*

# Foreword

*Healing Laughter*, A Dance for Breast Cancer Survivors answers two questions that the title itself invokes: What is healing laughter? and why is laughter a dance for breast cancer survivors?.

Seriously, why would Connielee Smith write a book about a non-serious topic such as laughter? and how valuable laughter really is for such a gravely serious disease?

This special, powerful little book, answers these questions with both Biblical references, science based evidence and living proof that Connielee witnessed firsthand about the contrasting choices that laughter made for her family.  One of Connielees's sisters embraced healthy laughter when diagnosed with cancer and Connielee's other sister also diagnosed with cancer wasn't able to embrace laughter and joy. Connielee shares with you how her sister's choices affected everyone in her family that she will long remember.

The concept that laughter provides a healthy advantage after a diagnosis of breast cancer may seem counter intuitive to many of us since breast cancer isn't funny or humorous.  However, by engaging in laughter in our daily lives, we are less susceptible to falling deeper into the throes of depression, sadness, hopelessness, and the negative emotional vortex of breast cancer, that emotional energy vampire that robs us moment by moment, day by day from the joys of living until we are separated from the best feelings of life.

As a breast cancer survivor, Connielee knows that there are days we don't feel like laughing and someone popping an untimely or insensitive joke might be upsetting, not uplifting. Yet, building a relationship with laughter and joy becomes a choice for quality of life. With healthy laughter, relationships can be mended, healthy endorphins are released in the body, and our spirits are lifted.

Let us all engage in what Connielee calls healthy laughter when we can and while we can.  Let the compassion, kindness, and wisdom of Connielee's words help you and your family to embrace the best of life and the best of each other.

May faith, love, laughter, and joy be powerful allies in your healing journey.

*Beverly Vote*
*Publisher, TheBreast Cancer Wellness Magazine*

# **Dedication**

To my wonderful husband who supported me all of the way.

To my precious mom who has always believed I could do it.

To my grandchildren who gave me a huge reason to stick around.

Abby, Lexi, Carson, Emma, and Natalie:

I love you more than the best chocolate in the whole world!

# Introduction

Life was good. My husband and I were looking forward to retirement at last! We wanted to travel around the country and "see the sites." Route 66 was calling me, so I bought a book all about it. That was pretty exciting for someone as untraveled as I was.

Our two daughters had married and started their own families. Visiting our grandchildren was definitely in the plan. We were ready, or so I thought.

I am very careful about getting a mammogram every year along with the annual checkup. I had lost two sisters to cancer, so I couldn't afford to forget. That rainy November morning I went to my doctors' office, had my exam and breezed out of the building. All was well. Next was the dreaded mammogram. They are dreaded because no matter how many a woman has, they still hurt! Since my breasts were fibrous the tech had to really give my girls an extra squeeze before it was done.

I sat in a little cubby waiting to hear if I could go home. Instead the tech came in and told me the radiologist wanted me to have an ultrasound. They had seen something on the films that concerned them. I was scheduled for the ultrasound after lunch that very day.

This wasn't the first dance with that. Years earlier I had an excisional biopsy. The surgeon removed the mass, had it checked and all was well, it was benign. Yes, I know, pretty awesome! This ultrasound didn't turn out the way I had hoped.

I was alone with my thoughts, while the tech talked to the radiologist. I was beginning to get a really sick feeling in the pit of my stomach. Now, I was worried.

Over 800 women are diagnosed with breast cancer every day. In one year over one-quarter million women will have been told they have cancer. That statistic is staggering when considering that many women were in their 20's when diagnosed, younger than ever. I was 57 and thought I had dodged the bullet.

I went to lunch and came back. The ultrasound tech was a nice young man and it went just fine. He too saw something and went to find the doctor. It didn't take a rocket scientist to figure there was something very wrong with one or both of my breasts.

The doctor came and said they needed to do a biopsy in the office. I had no idea what that meant, I do now. Without grossing any of you dear readers out, it was 6 snips of what was a mass in my left breast. When done, the doctor just patted my shoulder and said we could pray that it would come out ok. Seriously? What does that exactly mean? Are you expecting it not to be ok?

Later that day, my doctor called and told me that it was cancer and I would need to see a surgeon right away. He hung up and I just stood there with the phone in my hand.

## GOD IS THERE

That night as my husband slept, I was wide awake with the what-ifs. Nothing good ever comes from that game. If you find yourself playing it, stop immediately and focus on something positive and good in your life or your family. It was at that moment when God reminded me that He had promised to never leave me and that He would always be with me.(Proverbs 14:30,Hebrews 13:5) In the darkness God and I talked. Actually, I talked and He listened. I poured out my heart and soul to Him. I didn't ask why, but I wondered why three girls out of four in my family had to do the cancer dance. It really didn't matter. The fact was that I would be busy the next several months staying alive. God has always been a part of my life. His promises in the scripture have given me strength I didn't know possible. I give Him credit for the courage and resolve that I found that night. While going through the maze of appointments and such, I was amazed at the calm that had begun to dwell within my very being.

Our journeys are all unique to each of us. We choose different treatment options and perhaps choose to be treated outside the medical community. Yet, at the same time, we all face some of the same fears and concerns.

Having said that, I found in my journey the need to keep my joy intact and rather than be depressed I wanted to be able to find something to laugh about. Later on I will share about my two sisters who had cancer. One chose to be unhappy while the other chose to find something that would keep her smiling. It's a choice that we each will make and it is my greatest hope that you will choose joy.

"Sometimes your joy is the source of your smile,
but sometimes your smile is the source of your joy."

— *Thich Nhat Hanh*

⤴ JILL ⤵

One of my favorites was the breast MRI. I was belly
down, boobs through the holes, and the technician was
underneath tugging and positioning them. I let out a
huge moooooo. Good times. Also, when I tell people I had
breast cancer I would say: "I have good news, and I have
bad news." The bad news is I have breast cancer. The
good news is that I'm seeing a hot plastic surgeon who
keeps asking me to take my shirt off."

# { Chapter 1 }

# WHY SHOULD I LAUGH? IT'S HEALING

Over the past 50 years there have been numerous studies within the medical world about the benefits of laughter. The late Norman Cousins, writer for the Saturday Review, is considered to be the "Father of the Mind-Body Connection." He believed that the brain responded to the body and its' emotions. This is true for both positive and negative emotions. For our purpose we will discuss the power of laughter and its' benefits.

At an early age Cousins was able to see the differences between people with hope and people who had no hope. He contracted Tuberculosis as a boy and was put in a Sanitorioum. He would go out to hang with other boys and noticed something interesting.There were two distinct groups. One group of boys just wandered around, not playing or having fun. The other group of boys liked to play kick ball, run, jump, and do whatever they could to have fun together. He called the first group fatalists. These boys felt they were going to die so why do anything? The second group would be the optimists. They might die, but wanted to play and have fun until it happened. Years later, Mr. Cousins looked back on that time and found that most of the fatalists did indeed die in the Sanitorium.

In 1994 Cousins was diagnosed with Ankylosing Spondylitis. This meant that the connective tissue in his spine was deteriorating. It was an extremely painful condition for which there was no treatment, let alone cure.

He began his own research and found that his condition was depleting his body of Vitamin C. He convinced his doctors to take him off all medications, but to inject him with a large dose of Vitamin C. He then got a movie projector and a large supply of funny films, including the Marx Brothers and Candid Camera. He watched these and laughed until he cried. After ten minutes he found he could sleep without pain for up to two hours. When the pain returned, he would begin watching the programs again. He was able to measure the inflammation and infection in his blood. Mr. Cousins found that the rate dropped by at least 5 points each time he would watch these videos.

How did that work? The body is laughing and the brain begins releasing all sorts of wonderful things for your body to use like dopamine and endorphins — giving you a kind of laughing high. These hormones block pain. Our brains also release more immune cells than normal. These trusty cells help aid in the healing of diseases. I don't claim that they heal disease. Norman Cousins felt that laughter was indeed a great medicine, in complement to medical care. Also, laughter causes stress to be eased, bonding to occur as people laugh together, and the opening up of the blood vessels to the heart; thereby increasing the blood flow and protecting the heart. Laughter can heal relationships.

Cousin wrote about prominent men throughout history who knew about the healing power of laughter. This list included Sir Frances Bacon, Sigmund Freud and Albert Schweitzer. This wasn't a new hypothesis. Men throughout history had proven laughter's effectiveness!

This is not a book about promises to heal. It is a book about allowing your joy to help you along the path towards healing. Joy or laughter can be cathartic spiritually, emotionally, socially, and physically. Throughout the book there are stories about breast cancer survivors who chose joy over sadness or depression. Read them over and over again. I know you will feel the joy in the hearts of these women who have gone through cancer and come out on the other side. Feel free to laugh with us as we tell you our stories. This is a book for you to enjoy and then perhaps pass along to someone who might be needing encouragement and laughter.

My Girls are gone

### ꊛ BRENDA ꊛ

Humor and laughter are so important. So much of going through treatments is a downer so anytime you can laugh it helps you feel better. I had several friends who helped me laugh a lot. One friend had just finished her treatments as I started mine. She was so helpful.

# { Chapter 2 }

# MAKING SENSE OF CHAOS

I don't know what your mind did when you heard those two words, "its cancer." My mind turned into a radio that had way too many channels tuned in at one time.

I began to worry about my family, death, finances, insurances, my hair, second opinions, etc. Did you?

That's a normal response to something as overwhelming as a cancer diagnosis. When given any information, our minds will somehow tune into all the possibilities and we try to make some sense of it. When given information with countless ramifications, our minds turn into chaos. As with most things in life, it is easier to deal with one thing at a time. I want to encourage you to take those concerns and put them on paper. List them as you think of them. Separate the lists into 3 columns. One would be personal, one would be medical, and one would be financial. Are you able to do this? As you list things, you will find that not all of your concerns can be addressed yet. It will take more time to get the information you need to make decisions. Show this list to your mate or a good friend. Sometimes it helps when someone can voice your concerns and help you put some of them in perspective. It might be awhile before all the chaos settles down.

For me, it was much easier because I had walked with my sisters through much of the process. I also surfed the Internet and educated myself. I wrote down any and all questions I had. Don't be afraid to ask your doctor. He is there to make this whole experience easier for you.

If you are comfortable with meditation or even yoga it might help to get back into the practice as you feel you can. Quiet times can be useful for rest, getting yourself centered, get more control of your emotions. Self-talk is really good too. It might work better if you're alone so people don't think you have an invisible friend with whom you are conversing. I have been known to talk myself out of a funk. I've talked myself out of bed in the morning several times. Our conversations with ourselves can be enlightening too. Have you ever listened to how you talk to you? Seriously, be nice to you, encourage you, inspire you. Don't be mean or denigrating about who you are. You are perfect as God made you. It can't get any better than that. Don't be afraid to name your feelings and emotions. This is just between you and you. No one else needs to be privy to your conversations. Build yourself up.

## A peaceful heart leads to a healthy body.

*— Proverbs 14:30*

Remember that during this time of chaos, you will have many emotions playing through your head. That's alright. As you begin to digest the diagnosis your brain will begin to settle and this is the time to find your joy if it's gone, or maintain it throughout this maze we call cancer.

## "Be happy for this moment, this moment is your life."

*— Anonymous*

chaos
what to do?

## ⤳ RAMONA ⤳

I truly believe laughter is the best medicine for what ails you. Two long time girlfriends made a party out of shaving my head; eventually I would have no hair on my body. I really enjoyed not having to shave my pits and legs, but it was a bit difficult to find where my eyebrows where supposed to go.

I requested a friend to bring me barbecue for lunch during a chemo treatment. It was so good! I had to laugh when the result was diarrhea the next day. Someone who hasn't been there doesn't seem to understand the humor.

# { Chapter 3 }

# LEARNING TO LAUGH

## THE UNHEALTHY LAUGH

Have you ever been around someone who continually makes jokes about themselves? They seem to need to put themselves down and laugh while doing it. This is what I mean by unhealthy laughter.

Two types of unhealthy laughter:

1. Laughing to put yourself down.
2. Laughing to cover up pain.

People who put themselves down have most likely been teased about that very thing. The person jokes about it to get the jump on someone who might be thinking about laughing at him/her.

When you see that happening and you know them well, let them know that you don't like it when they put themselves down, you like them just the way they are.

Laughter can also be used to cover up pain. During the past several years there have been a few well-known comedians take their own lives. For example, while they laughed and made us laugh, there was something deep inside that was hurting. They didn't share their hurt with anyone; not even family. As the burden becomes unbearable, they feel the need to get away from it all. Laughter can cover a multitude of emotions. Pain, sadness, depression, fear, and anxiety are just a few that can be covered by laughter. This is not healthy. Don't allow yourself to bury your negative emotions behind a laugh. Be honest and get the help you need.

## HEALTHY LAUGHTER

I love to hear my grandchildren laughing as they play outside. There is such an innocence and true joy to be heard. Many situation comedies of the 1960's through 1980's were written for the purpose of causing laughter. A few of those that were on TV were: I Love Lucy, The Red Skelton Show, and The Carol Burnett Show. The comedy on these shows could bring a viewer to tears from laughing. Do you remember the last time you laughed until you had tears running down your face?

I tend to laugh a lot, so I want to share the first time I laughed until I cried.

Our family attended a small church. The church pews were wooden, and not very comfortable. One of the families attending the church always sat in the second row on the right side. There was the dad and son, mom and daughter. This little gal was just a doll. She always had ringlets in her long hair and wore the cutest outfits. One evening, after church had started and the pastor began his sermon, we heard this awful, echoing sound coming from the second row. I wasn't very old at the time, but I knew that someone had passed some gas. The first thing I did was look at my mom. She had her head down and was trying very hard not to laugh. I heard her whisper, "don't laugh." That's about all she wrote, folks. It hit me funny and I started laughing. I looked at my sister, which was a big mistake, and she was laughing too. Her laughs were quiet, but her body was shaking and tears were running down her face. By this time, the mom in the second row was so mortified by her daughter's gas that she was about ready to crawl under the pew. That didn't bother me, because I was beyond help at the point. We could hear snickers around the sanctuary, but no one was going to be caught laughing out loud, especially the older saints. Now, my mom had told me not to laugh, I paid the ultimate price for laughing. My mom slapped my bare leg (not hard) so all could hear the smack. That was a small price to pay for such cleansing laughter.

This incident happened so many years ago, yet when I asked my mom if she remembered, she did, just like it was yesterday. It wasn't so much about the little girl. It was really about the laughter my sister and I shared. She is gone now, so I can't laugh with my sister anymore. This memory keeps her alive.

Laugh with joy and thanksgiving. Laugh because you can. Laugh when you're by yourself reading a great book. Laugh at nature around you. Remember to laugh for joy, not from pain.

> "We don't see things as they are;
> we see things as we are."
>
> *– Anais Nin*

## ⟿ MARY ANN ⟿

There is a time to laugh and a time to cry. I remembered
one time I asked the ladies in my support group in
Houston to tell me a time either of laughing or crying.
One told of driving from College Station, Texas to
Houston. Her friend was in the front seat, her son in the
back seat. A couple of Texas Aggies pulled alongside them
and started flirting, tipping their cowboy hats to her. She
fell back a bit and her son said, "Mom, do it." She knew
what he meant, so she caught up with them and they
looked over at her just as she tipped her wig to them.
That did it, they then fell back.

Another woman told of how she and a number of friends
were in a hot tub when her wig fell off and she put it
back on. The trouble was that it was on backward!

# { Chapter 4 }

# LAUGHTER YOGA

It is only recently that I have become acquainted with this type of yoga. One of our pink sisters wrote about attending a camp for breast cancer survivors with Laughter Yoga.

There is not a huge amount of information out there, but I did find a few tidbits and hopefully some direction should you be interested trying this. Laughter Yoga actually began in India in 1995. It caught on and is in a lot of countries around the world. The United States has embraced Laughter Yoga. Hospitals, Industry, Elder Care, Cancer Centers, Senior Centers, and Centers for the Disabled now use it as a way of relieving stress and anxiety among their people.

The premise for Laughter Yoga is the same as Mind Body Connection. Our brain does what our body needs. The main difference that I see is that it is believed that our bodies can't tell the difference between faked laughter and real laughter as long as the participant is willing and eager to try Laughter Yoga.

Laughter Yoga doesn't seem to be for the faint of heart, or maybe it is. You decide. It is said to bring the introverted person into a socially accepting group. Feeling this acceptance allows them to participate along with others without feeling awkward.

I can't speak to the validity of Laughter Yoga as I have not tried it. I am relating what I have found so you will know about this option for helping with laughter. If you have lost your laughter or are having a difficult time with it, perhaps this might work.

If indeed the brain can't tell the difference between a fake laugh and a real laugh, then after about 10 minutes of laughing one would begin to feel the effects of it. Endorphins and dopamine would be released into your body. You would feel less pain, stress and anxiety. Some people say that happens when they participate.

One interesting description of Laughter Yoga is "Internal Jogging." Yes, you read that right! I'm just thinking about my insides doing a lap around the track and had to chuckle. The laughter for this discipline of Yoga is not a gentle chuckle or social giggle. This laughter is a gut busting, knee-slapping, gully washing belly laugh. It is a laugh from deep within the person. It is a laugh of joy and appreciation. How long has it been since you laughed like that? If you don't know, but want to do it, this may be something to pursue.

The Yoga portion of this is basically the breathing portion. There is a guided deep breathing and at the end there is a time for feeling your body relax as you might in a yoga class.

These classes all have exercises to do in each session. I'm not talking about jumping jacks or sit ups. I am talking about being able to set up situations in which you might use laughter. It is the goal of this class to make your fake laughter eventually turn into true laughter.

One example of an exercise I read about in a downloaded pamphlet is the cell phone laugh. The participant would pretend to be holding a cell phone in one hand, pretending to have a conversation with the person on the other end of the phone. At the same time you would be waving your other arm around as if you would be doing in person. Now it's time to be looking around and laughing on occasion at other people who are in the class. The laugh may be silent or loud.

While writing this chapter I had the opportunity to visit with yoga instructor, Diana Delacerna. She has taught yoga for several years at the local Community College.

Diana didn't really get acquainted with Laughter Yoga until she was diagnosed with leukemia several years ago. She had sought alternative treatment that was non-drug and adhered to a healthy lifestyle. She began to teach Laughter Yoga after that as a source of well-being and positive outlook. Laughter Yoga helps people remain positive and joyful in their lives regardless of circumstances. Diana is doing well and keeping so busy she is no longer able to teach classes in Laughter Yoga.

I also found that, Center Treatment Centers of America have integrated this into their therapies. It is called Laughter Therapy. They encourage both patient and family to be involved in this exercise. Children with cancer benefit greatly in having the therapy with their families. Many other hospitals throughout the world are integrating this into therapy sessions.

There are countless Laughter Yoga Clubs to be found. Many classes meet on a weekly basis. In India they meet daily. It is felt that laughter should be constant each day.

If this interests you, there are plenty of sites on the web. Before you get involved, check with your doctor first.

## ⌒ HEATHER ⌒

After 11 years of breast cancer you definitely need to
laugh a lot! Sometimes people don't understand how I
use humor to heal and cope, but it certainly helps me
and that's all that matters. I had a radical mastectomy
on my left side at age 32. I tell every nurse who gives my
mammogram on the right side that my mammogram
should really be half-price all things considered.You can
imagine the reaction I get. It comforts me not to take
everything seriously. It has gotten me this far so I'm
going to stay with it.

# { Chapter 5 }

# CHOOSING TO LAUGH

Laughter is a choice. Many times laughter can have a healing effect on all those in the same room as well as the person who is laughing. True laughter makes a difficult situation doable. You can't always laugh out loud, but you can chuckle. My husband chuckles a lot when he reads the funnies. On the other hand if I see a funny comic strip, I laugh out loud. We are all unique in our responses. The point is that you can laugh even when things aren't looking bright. There are always things around us to bring laughter. Your sense of humor will go a long way during some of these really uncomfortable tests.

When I was having the biopsy I got a bit queasy. I tried to take deep breaths so I would feel better. That wasn't working. I looked at this young man at the ultrasound machine and said I wasn't feeling well and couldn't remember how to deep breathe. He told me that deep breathing wouldn't help. Doctors have found that breathing like I was in labor would better help me relax. He then asked me if I know how to breathe like that? No, I didn't know how. I had C-Section births and that wasn't a part of the procedure. I had to ask him to show me how; that was humbling. This young man proceeded to show me how to breathe like I was in labor. He-He – Ho-Ho, etc. I still smile when I think about this. What a guy! He saved me from myself that day.

Over the years I have had several IVs and had blood drawn. Usually, there isn't a problem. Not my favorite thing, but doable, until now. With all due respect to nurses, I got a nurse without a sense of humor. That was not good, not good at all. She came with all of the paraphernalia necessary to place an IV. My arm was ready. Imagine my surprise when she didn't go to my arm, but stayed at the foot of the bed. I didn't know what was happening so I began to watch her very closely. It was when she took an alcohol pad and was cleaning the top of my foot that I started losing it.

In my scared, squeaky voice I asked her what she was doing. Without skipping a beat she says, and I quote, "I'm getting ready to put the IV in your foot." Now my alarm bells are going off and I automatically pull both feet up to my chest and told her, and I quote again, "I don't think so." She gave me two options for the IV and one was not my arm. I could have it in my neck (Really?) or my foot, it was my choice, hmmm, what to do. Actually I only had one choice because there was no way on God's green earth there would be a needle in my neck.

Then, this incredible look of understanding crossed her face, it was fast, but I saw it. The nurse realized I hadn't been told about this very special IV. Because both breast were going to be done the IV needed to be in the foot.

"Oh, poop," I though. Now I had to stretch my short leg out and give her my foot. Mercy, to say its hurt would be a tremendous understatement of monumental proportions. I hope you understand my meaning. Ripping my foot off my ankle couldn't have hurt as much. I'm sure everyone on that floor of the hospital heard this poor little woman croaking "Ow, Ow Ow" for the next several minutes. I was so upset I asked for a barf bag because I thought I might barf.

A few minutes after she finished, the operating nurse came to take me to the bathroom. Okay, are you kidding me? You couldn't have come, like twenty minutes ago, before I was trussed up? Luckily, I got to stay in my bed for the short ride around the corner. In her sweet voice she asks: "Did they let you hang your foot down over the side of the bed?" I numbly shook my head no, they hadn't. According to her they were supposed to because blood goes to the foot and can make the veins on the top of the foot swell. I turned around to see if the nurse with no humor was around. Lucky for her — she wasn't.

I was still in pre-op when a very young man came into my cubby. This youngster was carrying a mighty big needle. Let me just say that he looked about 16-years-old. He wanted to put dye in my breasts. All I could think was "you've got to be kidding me — are you old enough?" However, I didn't say any of that. I bravely let him do what he needed to do. I was pretty embarrassed as a straight-laced 57-year-old woman. This was a first and only time I hope to have to do that. I did chuckle after he left.

Getting Shot

Mom and Loren (my husband) came back in and I told them about my experience. My mom got a good laugh from the story. Pretty soon he came back to wheel me down to radiology to check if the dye had worked its' way through the breast tissue. I guess you know by now that nothing is turning out as good as I had hoped, so no, it hadn't. As I laugh writing this,

I remembered being mortified when I was asked to massage my breast to move the dye around. I wasn't quite sure I heard them right. Something about that seemed so wrong. Because I am a strait-laced middle-aged woman the word "perversion" ran through my tiny brain. My eyes were as big as saucers, but I managed to give it a go. All I could think about was if Jesus comes will I be left for doing this. Not really, but it was stressful to say the least.

After that things went well. They wheeled me into the operating room and I asked them to turn the heat up and turn the lights down because they were hurting my eyes! I always needed to keep the humor moving.

These two situations could have gone differently. I could have refused to work with the techs. I could have cried and thrown a fit out of pain and fear. Choosing to laugh and take it in stride made it easier for me to endure the discomfort of the procedures.

Earlier I mentioned the benefits of laughter. Laughter did relieve stress and it did provide me with the strength to continue. I didn't break out in loud laugh. It was more like an inner thought of how very interesting life is and could it get any better?

## CATERPILLAR OR BUTTERFLY? WHICH ARE YOU?

Two of my sisters had cancer. Brenda had breast cancer and Sharon had ovarian cancer. Looking back I can see the different ways each sister dealt with their diagnosis.

Brenda was diagnosed at Stage IV Metastatic breast cancer. The doctors tried chemotherapy, but the cancer was just too advanced. Brenda only lived 5 months after she was diagnosed. This was 20 years ago. So much has changed with treatments that are now available. During those few months we spent time laughing and teasing each other. She really enjoyed teasing mom. She didn't laugh all the time, but when she could, she would break out her beautiful smile. Brenda wanted to take communion so my sister, Julene Edmond, a minister, brought her communion and they took it together. After she was done, Brenda said "I feel slickery." That meant she felt good.

One day a dear friend of ours, Kelle Schott brought a home baked pie over to the house. We sure enjoyed that pie. I do mean we enjoyed as much as we could eat. Later that afternoon while we were resting, Brenda calls down the hallway "Does your stomach hurt as much as mine does?" Groaning, I answered yes. Brenda replied "It was sure good pie though, wasn't it." "Yep, it was." Then I heard her sweet chuckle. Her body regretted eating so much pie, but her heart delighted in the experience!

Brenda chose to laugh! She had every reason not to. Doctors had ignored her complaints for months. As she lost her ability to eat or walk someone finally listened. It was too late for her to have any chance of survival. She could have been angry and hard to deal with. Brenda chose to live each moment that she had. Her death broke my heart.

I was not very good in science, but I do remember the green caterpillar that would spin its' cocoon and when it was time would break out as a beautiful butterfly. As cancer survivors we can choose not to spin the cocoon and be miserable, or we can spin that cocoon and come out of the experience a beautiful butterfly.

Sharon was diagnosed with ovarian cancer around 1998. She was able to be part of trials for her first diagnosis and she went into remission. During her treatments we had great times. We talked recipes, treats, kids, and whatever else we could think of. Our room became the social hub of the nurses. It was a positive experience for all of us.

During her year of remission, her husband passed away from cancer. When her cancer returned she didn't have her husband to go with her and didn't want the sisters there either. She closed herself off from people and went to all her chemo and radiation treatments by herself. Only as she began to weaken did she allow others to help. Sharon was sad and just couldn't find her joy that she once had. For 6 more years she fought cancer. During those years we were pretty solemn around her. It was hard to visit with her because we needed to be careful of what we said and how it was said. She didn't want to celebrate holidays like she used to before Morey died. Years before we used to go to her house to see what wonderful décor she had put out. Our laughs made her feel we had forgotten that she had cancer. During these years her relationship with mom was healed. She would often call mom and apologize for something she did as a girl. She loved my mom and did lean on her. She died the day after Thanksgiving in 2007. It was more difficult than words can say to tell her goodbye knowing she had not been able to find that joy again. I do know that she still loved Jesus and was going to heaven, but her death was somber. Family relationships were strained beyond saving. There was no joy or laughter to be found among several family members. During her illness, Sharon wanted to be alone much of the time for reasons of her own. She had some friends at her church she visited with. Her sadness was contagious. "For the happy heart, life is a continual feast." Proverbs 15:15b

The choice to have joy and laughter is yours and yours alone. As you refuse to laugh so must your family as they spend time with you. Your choices affect everyone around you.

> "What the caterpillar calls the end of the world,
> the master calls a butterfly."
>
> *–Richard Bach*

# { Chapter 6 }

# LAUGH ANYWAY

It doesn't take long in this life to learn that things don't always turn out the way we planned. Sometimes it's better, sometimes not so much. The key to making it work whichever way it happens is to keep a sense of humor about it. It's important not to take ourselves too seriously and not to take life too seriously. Our lives are given to enjoy the creation around us, families and friends, and the beauty of life itself.

Matthew 11:28 says: Then Jesus said, "Come to me, all of you who are weary and carrying heavy burdens and I will give you rest." We are beckoned by Jesus to let Him have the things that hurt us, scare us, and even intimidate us. Releasing our burdens to Him allows us to enjoy this life that we have been given, even when things go wrong.

I decided to have a TRAM Flap reconstruction about a year after I finished treatment. I had gotten really tired of wearing prostheses, which I will address later. I went to a surgeon who had a great deal of experience with this procedure. It is a major surgery. Since I had a bilateral mastectomy I knew it would be a time consuming surgery. The day came for it and I was ready. I was pretty excited about having two breasts again. Size wasn't a big deal to me. During surgery the blood flow died in the right breast. The micro-surgeon spent two hours to try to fix it. That didn't happen. My surgeon had to close the right breast and return it to a flat area.

When I came out of surgery my husband whispered to me "you only got one." I had been under for over twelve hours and was heavily sedated. I had no idea what one thing I got and why that was a problem. The doctor had tried to explain it the night before but I wasn't very aware of anything and couldn't understand him either. I was very out of it. After a long nap I asked my husband what was going on. He told me what had happened. Surprisingly, I wasn't that upset about it. My surgeon was. He was apologizing all the time for it and wouldn't let anyone else change the dressings. I know he felt bad as a young surgeon. I finally told him it was ok that it happened. I didn't want it to die after it was already a part of my body. If it was going to die, before it got on my body was better. I think perhaps he was taken aback by my outlook.

To Boob or Not to Boob
The old one, two.

I could have been angry. I could have made his life miserable. What would have been gained? He was already so miserable he could hardly look at me. So, I only had one breast. That was doable, I might be a bit lopsided, but I could take care of that.

I did have a sort of spiritual happening one of the nights in the ICU. Do you know the story of Samuel and Eli? It is a story in the Old Testament (1 Samuel 3) about an old priest and a young boy. God speaks to this young boy and tells him wonderful things. He goes to Eli and tells him about the voice.

I want to pick my own story up there. I hope you can see this happening in your mind. I was asleep and all of the sudden I heard a voice booming, "Connie, you aren't breathing deep enough." I looked around the room and there was no one to be seen. I dozed a bit, again the voice boomed, Connie, can you put the oxygen back up to your nose?" OK. I was pretty sure I was awake and hadn't died, but where was that voice coming from. I took a good look and still I was all alone in my room. That felt a bit eerie. About two minutes later a nurse came walking into my room and wanted to take care of the oxygen problem. Finally I got it! She was the voice. They had televisions to check on us in the ICU. God had not spoken aloud to me and I was a little disappointed. I had begun to think that God might actually be a woman. It's a good thing to have a sense of humor when things aren't going your way. You might have to look hard, but find something that isn't all bad and be happy about that.

Back in my journey I had been fitted by a "certified" fitter. I will say she may have been certified, but not in fitting prostheses. I came out wearing major boobs! Take them off and use as a slingshot, someone would be going down! When I went to the doctor, they did not go with me. I think they weighed more than my real girls.

We went camping with my daughter and her family shortly after that. We had a tent and I was trying to sleep in a bit. My little granddaughter had other ideas. She came bouncing into the tent to wake me up. In her little girl way she wanted to help me get dressed. Her mommy is very slight built while I am a bit more rounded. Abby bent over to pick up my bra for me to put on. Immediately this look of confusion came onto her little face. She knew about bras but didn't know they come pre-filled. She quietly put the bra down and turned around and bounded out of my tent. I laughed until I cried. It was precious time with family. I could have been embarrassed and snapped at Abby. I chose to laugh, after she left the tent. Memories are great things to have, greats memories are better.

Wonder Boobs
Lethal Weapons

**"The most wasted of all days is one without laughter."**

*— eecummings*

# { **Chapter 7** }

# LAUGHING THROUGH THE "FOG"

Chemo Brain. I had heard the term, but didn't truly appreciate what it meant, until I got it. To begin with, be aware that if you didn't have chemotherapy, you don't have chemo brain. See your doctor if these symptoms describe you. People who have had radiation on their brains may also suffer from this fog.

If you have had chemo, then these symptoms will help you know if you have chemo brain.

### Short Term Memory Loss

Before chemo I had the memory of all memories. I never forgot things, places, or people. Now if it's not written down it's not going to be remembered.

### Trouble Paying Attention

Some people naturally have problems with this. They are naturally a bit antsy, always on the move. Sitting still is not one their traits. I used to read books constantly. Now I rarely finish a book because I can't stay focused long enough.

## Trouble Finding the Right Word

My husband has now become my interpreter/translator. There are days when I should not talk! Nothing comes out right and my husband helps me out. He has become a genius at finishing my sentences as well. It is good to have someone you can rely on to help out when you have a day like that. You want someone who won't be laughing at you the entire day. My husband actually takes it more seriously than I do sometimes.

## Difficulty With New Learning

I used to knit and crochet. After treatment I wanted to start doing it again. I bought some beautiful and expensive yarn and all the other things I thought I might need to get going on a project. I sat down and realized I had forgotten how to knit or crochet. I was so upset that I put everything away and wouldn't look at it again for a long time. I got antsy, so I bought a book on easy knitting. I figured the word easy would do it for me. I worked so hard to remember. Being left-handed didn't help because illustrations were right-handed. People say that I can do it the opposite way. Really? Years earlier I could have figured it out, but there was this blank spot right in the middle of my brain that couldn't get it done. The yarn is once again put up and ready for a third try.

## Difficulty Managing Daily Tasks

Some of us are naturally disorganized and can't blame chemo brain for it. Sorry if that's you. Bummer! I will say that many years ago before children, my home was almost spotless. I had kids and it wasn't for several years. Kids grow up and leave; my house is still not clean. I can't really blame chemo brain although I would like to. It would be fair to say that I can't keep things picked up around the house. It just kind of sits there and stays there. If I try to do too much then nothing gets done. Here is a gem that my doctor shared with me. Do one thing; just try to accomplish one thing in the day. That bit of encouragement changed my entire outlook. The fog didn't have to win. I could do just one thing and win. If this will help you, please give it a try. You won't feel that frustration you might have felt at seeing so little accomplished. Some days the fog will be more noticeable than others, that's normal and give yourself some room to deal with it however you can. Don't start new projects on those days or set unrealistic goals. Take it easy and maybe get some extra rest. Go for a walk with someone; go for coffee, or just journal.

**Confusing Days and Appointments**

If you once had a steel trap for a mind and now it has become a sieve, then you might find yourself mixing up dates, doctor appointments, which doctor to see, or even the time for you appointment. How frustrating that can be. There is hope for you. It's called a day keeper or even a calendar on your phone or wall in your kitchen. Take it with you when you make appointments and write them down as soon as you make them. Please do that before you leave the office. You will feel better and be in control of at least this part of your life.

If you struggle with these symptoms the first thing you need to do is let your doctor know. Your doctor needs to be aware of what is happening in your life. If you have a lot of really foggy, slow days, he needs to know. You might need some type of medication to balance your brain. Be honest with family and friends when you are having a foggy day. They need to be aware so that you will be safe and they can help you accomplish your errands. Remember not to drive on those days. Take your friends up on their offers and get a ride with someone. It is ok to lean on your family and friends. They want to help and would be thrilled if you let them.

I want to encourage you to keep a journal to track your moods and feelings. You don't have to write pages and pages. Just write a sentence or two that would describe how you felt that day and if you were able to accomplish anything. This information would be good to have available for the doctor when you talk with him/her.

Most of the time, these symptoms are temporary. In fact, many will disappear shortly after chemo ends, while others may hang on for a while. One or two might stick with you indefinitely. You can deal with these possibilities because you have already dealt with hard things.

There was a time when doctors weren't as all sympathetic to women who complained of these problems. They thought it was all in their heads, and they were right, just not the way they thought they were. As the complaints began mounting and more women were having difficulties living their lives normally, the medical community finally woke up and decided that the complaints might have some validity. They began doing research to find out what caused the symptoms. Research showed that there were actual changes in the brain where the cognitive skills are located. One definition of cognitive would be mental sharpness. Doctors have actually given MRI's to women who had serious symptoms of chemo brain and it showed those physical changes in the brain.

The main problem for measuring the seriousness of chemo brain is that there is no type of pre-treatment test that is being done. So, many changes that are new wouldn't be shown as such because there was no way to know what the brain looked like beforehand. If your symptoms are really serious you might want to seek out a professional counselor or psychologist. I know that last word conjures all sorts of things in our minds. There are people who feel it is wrong to ever see a "shrink." All I can say to you is that these doctors are trained to help you develop skills to deal with whatever is troubling you. If I were truthful I would tell you that I see one every few months. The skills that I have developed have helped me in many areas of my life. I am not the same person I was before breast cancer. I see things differently, sometime it's nice to find out why and if it's a good thing. I like to know that there is someone I can talk to who I know will keep all I say confidential and work to help me be a better person. I won't say anything else about this, but know that if you go, you will learn many new things about yourself that you never knew!

When I am having a bad day I have my husband to help me. I just roll my eyes at him and say "chemo day." Those two words are all I need to say. He sticks close to me so I don't offend anyone or hurt myself. He is my daily strength here on earth. God is my strength during the night when I am alone and during the day He watches my steps.

Stay positive. Don't let chemo brain take you down into depression. You are strong and you can handle this. As they say, "You've got this." You are not defined by your fog or your lack of fog. It is just a small part of your life. There are so many things that make up the whole.

## THINGS THAT YOU CAN DO

Chemo Brain can actually be made worse by several things that you probably didn't give a second thought to.

I am just going to list them without saying much.

- Low blood count
- Stress and anxiety
- Depression
- Fatigue and sleep disturbances
- Hormone changes
- Medications to treat side effects

Your doctor needs to know if you are feeling any of these symptoms. These things can be treated to help you. You can learn skills to relieve the stress and anxiety. Depression needs to be acknowledged. It's important that you remain honest with your doctor and let him/her help you. You may find that chemo brain is not so severe once these have been taken care of.

## COPING STRATEGIES

Here are some things you can do to help cope with the foggy days.

**Exercise** – Start small and build up. Any type of exertion is good. It takes about 20 minutes of exercise for the brain to release the endorphins that help you feel better.

**Memory Aids** – Check with your oncologist to see if there are some available for you to use. If not, the internet has some excellent sites, such as Lumosity. It is a site that will reteach you how to do things that requires thought and skills of organization.

**Fatigue** – Fatigue by itself can cause a mental fog. If you don't sleep well or you wake up during the night, you will become fatigued. Again, let me encourage you to tell your doctor about your sleep patterns. Your mind may need to be retrained when to sleep.

Babies often get their schedules all mixed up. They will sleep during the day and want to play all night. It takes several days to retrain them, but it can be done. You can be retrained too. You might consider getting involved in a sleep study to find out why you're not sleeping.

**Depression** – I won't say much here as I have already mentioned it. I just want you to be aware that it can play a large part with chemo brain because depression causes one not to have energy or to even have hope. Don't lose your hope. Hope is necessary for life. Take the first step by telling your doctor.

We haven't laughed a great deal in this chapter. Chemo brain can have its' funny moments, but not very many; however you can take moments that might be stressful or full of anxiety and find something that will make it better. I tend to joke when I am stressed because that's how I handle it. You might handle it differently. Laughter needs to be a part of your life all the time, every day. Don't lose your ability to laugh.

On your good days why don't you get out and do something for someone. There are many places that need volunteers. Some places that usually need volunteers are: libraries, senior centers, cancer centers, hospitals, food closets, and soup kitchens. I am sure that you can come up with several more in your community. Giving back can help take your mind off your problems and allow you to touch someone's life for good.

Do you keep puzzles at home? Do you work crossword puzzles? Have you thought about taking a class, like yoga or cooking? Your choices are limitless.

You can do it. You are strong. You are a survivor.

No Hair Anywhere

Connielee as a 6-year-old with her family

L. to R.  Julene, Connielee. Mom, Brenda and Sharon

L. to R.  Julene, Connielee, Brenda and Sharon

Julene, Mom and Connielee

Connielee and husband, Loren

Our doxies, Henry and Charlie

In Seattle for Mom's 80th birthday

Connielee and Mom during Mom's first commercial flight

Holly Almond, CNP and Connie. She has been my doctor for the entire journey.

Loren and Connielee Walking for the Cure

Visiting family — still no hair, it was slow growing...

## ᴌ JULIE ᴌ

I went to a Laughter Yoga session at the Faces of Courage
Camp. It got me breathing deeply and smiling again for
the first time in months. Now I plug in online during
chemo. All the nurses are amazed that I laugh through
my weekly chemo session.

# { Chapter 8 }

# A NEW KIND OF LAUGHTER

Shortly after my hair was totally gone I took off my shirt and looked into the mirror. Oh, my goodness! I was a sight for sore eyes. Staring back at me was a 10-year old boy. I had no breasts, no hair, no brows, and no eyelashes. I barely recognized myself and was pretty sad about what I saw.

It was that day that I decided that a new me would be born through this experience. My body was a blank slate and anything was possible. It was kind of exciting to think about that.

As I've stated before, I am a conservative person by nature, but now I was ready to "live on the edge" — whatever that meant. I decided to get my eyebrows tattooed on and my eyeliner also. What an unusual thought for me. I found a wonderful Christian gal who has such a tender heart for breast cancer survivors. We worked together and within a few weeks I had eyebrows and eyeliner.

Shortly after that, my husband and I went on our first Breast Cancer Wellness Thrivers Cruise. It was wonderful and I felt like a million bucks with my makeup. I met so many pink sisters and have made friends for a lifetime. God has been faithful and provided friendships that have encouraged me and got me moving — rather than sitting around doing nothing.

I was also able to finish the breast reconstructions before the cruise. That step took three surgeries. I was tired of the hospital and needed a break.

I wore wigs and hats when my hair was gone. I also visited a website called Etsy.com and found many crafters who knit hats. I was able to make direct contact with one and chose the colors and size that I wanted. I still wear them because they are so beautiful.

I had only had one manicure before I was diagnosed with cancer. The chemotherapy did awful things to my nails so I started getting manicures. The nails became so thick that I couldn't file them. I began to have the gal put on green, blue, red, purple, and even dots on my nails. It has been so fun to be able to see my real nails and with the chemotherapy long over, have let my nails grow back to their natural shape and size. My poor toe- nails went through a rough time too. One of my baby toes lost its' nail.

I really felt like I was given a second chance to live and have been deter- mined to enjoy it and help others enjoy their second chances.

After all the treatments were done and my hair had come back it was time to close the book on this part of my life. The question was "*What did I want to do for the grand finale.*"

I had begun seeing articles about tattoos. I saw some beautiful designs. These women had chosen to have tattoos across their chests. Some had no breasts, some had one. Some had two breasts, but scarring, so they had a tattoo. These marvelous tattoos made a statement to me. They kind of said that each woman had kicked cancers' butt and came out stronger and more beautiful than before. I was hooked but didn't know how to go about the way of finding a place to get one. I didn't want to go to a parlor where other people could see what was going on. I searched the yellow pages for places that didn't have scary names. They were few and far between.

Then an amazing thing happened. One of the artists I spoke to referred me to a woman who had recently opened her own studio in her home. I got her web address and checked it out. Wow! Her work was amazing. The color and detail was so clear. I thought she could be the one to help me finish off this book. I made contact with her and she was willing to see what I had in mind. I found a design I liked and she made it mine. The design was cherry blossoms and I wanted a ribbon among the branches. The ribbon would be pink for Brenda and teal for Sharon. Linda was able to do everything and more than I could have thought possible.

My mom came with us when we checked out the studio. She loved the design and said "I think you should get a ladybug tattoo around your belly button."

My jaw dropped as my little 80-year-old mom said, "It's your body, own it."

Talk about being shocked, I was beyond shocked, but thrilled with her attitude. Looking back I'm not sure how I managed to sit for 4 or 5 hours at a time. I'm a pretty big wuss. Ask anybody who knows me and they will say I'm proud of my tattoo. *(See page 58)*

This tattoo makes me feel like a winner. There is a joy that wells up in my heart that God stayed with me through all of the ups and downs of breast cancer, just as He promised to do.

I know that most people might not want to go that far. That's ok. We all have unique and wonderful ideas of this. I want to encourage you to do something to celebrate your victory. Celebrate life. Celebrate joy.

"Tattoos are the stories in your heart,
written on your skin."

— *Charles De Lint, The Mysery of Grace*

## ꒰ LAKENIA ꒱

Humor is good for the mind, body and soul. When I tell
this story it has people in tears. I thought my biggest
obstacle would be my hair and cried at the mention of
losing it. When it began to come out, it started around the
lining of the front of my hair and I looked just like "Robo
Cop," literally. So, I named myself "ROBO LAKENIA," here
to save the day. Believe it or not, that helped me get over
the hump of losing my hair. When you can find humor in
what you are going through it lessens the load for those
around you, who don't really know what to say to make
it better. I know they are supposed to lift us up, but truth
be told, they are the ones who truly need the lift.

# { Chapter 9 }

# LET LAUGHTER REIGN

Now that treatment is over and your reconstruction, if chosen, is completed you might think it's time to get back to reality and knock the laughing off.

Fortunately for you, that isn't how it works. Surviving means that you made it through. That is certainly something to celebrate. What I want you to do is get stronger and thrive. A thriver is someone who continues to grow in strength and empathy.

Strength doesn't come on its own. If I wanted physical strength I would lift weights and work out on a regular basis. It's going to take some time and lots of work. As a thriver you will be able to encourage women who are facing breast cancer. You need to strengthen emotionally to be able to do this. Most encouragement for the breast cancer patients tends to meet more emotional needs.

Throughout this book I have shared many humorous stories. These stories might have ended differently, except for one thing: laughter. Laughter will always relax you when you're stressed, it will always help make the impossible tasks possible. Sometimes it's hard to laugh, I know. Through laughter you can find the strength within yourself. Your ability to continue to be joyful and have a great sense of humor will help you to see a future with a positive slant. Laughter will help you on the days that aren't too funny. Remember, the choice to laugh is yours.

Choose joy. Choose to see your life as a gift from God. His blessings have given you the chance to see potentials ahead where once you saw emptiness.

As you regain your strength, find someone you can encourage. Tell them how you made it through. It can be difficult to share with total strangers, but the returns far outweigh the effort put into the words. Not only will you continue to grow but the person you are encouraging is finding someone who understands and who has been in her shoes. She is finding someone who can answer some of her questions and calm her fears.

I hope you have laughed throughout this book as well as said "ouch" a couple of times. I pray you have learned the importance of having a joyful attitude when facing the mountain they call breast cancer.

## LAUGHTER IS INDEED THE BEST MEDICINE!

**DEAR PINK SISTER: THIS PAGE IS JUST FOR YOU!**

I've listed some ideas to create laughter. Most have been mentioned throughout this book, but I wanted to have a dedicated page just for these ideas. While your family and friends want to help, you can also come up with some things that you would like to do alone or with others.

These ideas will depend on your health and the area in which you live. If any of these are too ambitious please check with your doctor before you try them.

- Movie Rentals

    Many of the new animated movies are hilarious. Some of these might be: Ice Age, Madagascar, The Good Dinosaur, and Despicable Me. It is also possible to either rent TV series movies or get them through your On Demand program. Some of these TV Comedies are: I Love Lucy, Red Skelton, Carol Burnett, The Three Stooges, and The Marx Brothers. Remember, we want you to LAUGH.
- Comedy Clubs
- Laughter Yoga
- Karaoke
- Walking Groups
- Bowling
- Take a class in cooking, pottery, art
- Bingo
- Volunteer with children or senior citizens
- Zumba

Now, it is your turn. What do you like to do that is fun and makes you laugh? What is available in your city? Is there something you have always wanted to do, but haven't?

Fill in the lines with YOUR ideas and give yourself a boost. Be Brave!

1. _____

_____

_____

2. _____

_____

_____

3. _____

_____

_____

4. _____

_____

_____

5. _____

_____

_____

6. _____

_____

_____

Remember, pink sister, each day you choose how you want to feel. It is totally up to you. Laughter will help the undoable seem doable. It will make the awful seem not so bad. Laughter will also make you feel better. Take a step toward that laughter and see your future bright and full of adventure. You can do this!

_e_ WENDY _e_

When I had radiation treatments I had the best
therapists. They were both males and I used to call them
"The A Team." One time I was holding the "pose" and the
computer crashed and the therapists ask me to hold this
grotesquely uncomfortable pose for a long period of time.
While doing so I let out a loud fart. We were laughing so
hard and I said: "Breast Cancer keeps on giving and I just
had to share."

# { **Chapter 10** }

# NOTES TO FAMILY AND FRIENDS

You are in the unique position to help your loved one have a better journey than she might have. Breast Cancer is a devastating diagnosis for any woman and takes a while to digest. She might need quite a bit of time. I want to encourage you to give her some time to work through her feelings. Be there to listen or to share a cup of coffee.

By now, you know that I believe that joy or laughter is so important in the life of someone who is facing an extraordinary challenge like cancer. I want you to help your loved one remember that laughter makes the journey easier for everyone. A loss of laughter or a refusal to laugh can make the journey extremely difficult.

She may choose to pursue treatment that is not necessarily medically approved. There are so many treatments available today. Support her in her choices, even if you think it is the worst choice she has ever made. As long as she is sane and able to make her own decisions, accepting them with a smile will go a long way. Research her choices so you will be able to talk with her if she brings it up. Your research will help her know you are in her corner. This goes for family and friends. There is so much vocabulary that is impossible to understand let alone say, that it would be well to get some of that explained when possible.

You know her well and probably can tell when she is tired or troubled. It is important to be sensitive to those feelings. She might not be in the mood to laugh, be careful that you don't offend her by laughing too much around her. My sister believed that when we laughed, that meant we had forgotten that she had cancer. It wasn't true, but that is how she saw it.

Encourage her to be proactive. Don't wait for her hair to fall out, do something before it does should she have chemotherapy. Being proactive will help her feel more in control and ease some of the fears that might attack her in the night times.

All of you may have those night times when there is no one there but you and God. No one to talk to and no one tell about your fears. She will go through that too. That's normal. I'm pretty sure my mom had those each time one of her daughters was diagnosed with cancer.

Those times can be the most precious times you have with God. He wants you to tell Him how you feel. Tell Him about your fears. If you're angry, tell Him. Then spend some quiet time listening to Him. His Word contains so many promises that will bring peace to a fearful heart.

## Things NOT to say

Call me if you need anything.

Let me know if I can help.

Here's my number, give me a call.

By the way, my aunt had that and she died, but I'm sure her cancer was worse than yours.

Oh, you'll be just fine, up and around before you know and your kids will be such big helpers.

Now, be honest. Have you ever heard those words or even, gulp, said something like I mentioned? Don't worry. I think most of us have done so, unthinkingly. I was talking about this to a friend. She remarked that she had never given it any thought but now that we talked she would know a better way to help.

There is a better way. Those phrases above are called "shifting the pooh" to the patient. I used the term pooh because this a G rated book. I'm pretty sure you know what I mean.

We are asking a woman who has been through a pretty traumatic experience to take charge of her needs. We are asking her to bear the weight of finding help. That doesn't paint a very nice picture, does it?

I want to show you a better way to help; one that is precise and needs very little from your loved one.

## Things TO say

We are getting pizza this Wednesday, what time would be good to drop it off? I'll call before so we can get the order right.

Jenny would like for Susie to come over this week for a play date, would Thursday work? We'll bring her back after dinner.

I want to help with transportation to your therapy. I'll call you tomorrow so we can get a schedule.

Without saying anything, get a group together to help with yard work so her husband doesn't have too many things to accomplish.

Perhaps you could go together and have a professional give her house a deep clean even before she comes home, with permission from family, of course.

Offer to take her out for a drive and maybe a coffee the following week.

Do you see what I am doing? I am letting you take the responsibility off her shoulders. She doesn't want to be assailed all at once, but don't expect her to feel like making telephone calls.

You want to make this transition as easy as possible for her. Don't baby her, but give her some room to hurt, to cry, to complain, or just to sit and look out the window.

As much as my family helped, it was still a lonely journey inside. I was the one facing the treatment or surgery, or whatever. Their encouragement went a long way to help me get through the tough times.

Laughter will serve both you and your loved one well. Try to find things that she would enjoy seeing or reading. Tell stories that might tickle her.

As your loved one heals, you might consider hosting a tea for her and some close friends to catch up with one another. Another idea might be a hat party. She might be losing her hair and not have anything to put on her head. This could be a fun time of fashion and friendship. Brainstorm with friends about simple things to do that she might enjoy. It's important to be respectful of her feelings.

These few ideas will enable your loved one to get the assistance she needs without having to pick up the phone... that is what we all want for her.

## ～ KARI ～

I remember dying laughing because my best friend came over to help with the laundry and the hangers were all mixed up. As we were untangling them all, I made up this script like it was an infomercial "does this ever happen to you?" and I grabbed them all in the big jumbled mess and shook them like an idiot.

Another time we went to Target (me and my bestie) and we were taking the cart back inside the store. I jumped inside and she rolled the cart with me in it to the front of the parking lot. I remember a lot of stupid things like that. Mundane things turned funny in light of the seriousness of the situation.

# { Chapter 11 }

# MY FAMILY SPEAKS OUT

I took a chance and decided to ask my family if they would be willing to fill out a questionnaire about their feelings concerning my breast cancer diagnosis. I am living on the edge doing this. One never knows what a family member will say, but since I am now a risk taker I did it.

The questions were a bit different for each person, so some of these answers might not have three answers. My husband, mom, and one of my daughters completed the questionnaire. I hope you find is useful in understanding what your family and friends might be feeling. They might not want to share their feelings, but I think it's good to have insight.

## QUESTIONNAIRE

What was your first thought when you heard I had cancer?

Loren: I was shocked and wondered how it would play out.

Sarah: Oh, no. I'm not ready to lose my mom

Mom: Oh, no God, this can't be happening.


What was the hardest part for you during my treatment?

Loren: Seeing the effect of chemo on your body.

Sarah: Being so far away and not being able to do anything

Mom: To watch you go through long months of having surgeries and treatment and I couldn't help you.

### Did you feel good about the treatment I chose?

Loren: Yes. I thought it was the best option.

Sarah: Yes. I just wish it didn't have so many side effects.

### Did you have anybody to talk about your concerns during this time?

Loren: No

Sarah: Yes, Dustin

Mom: Yes, I talked to God more than ever. You and Loren were always very honest with me and told me what was going to happen. Julene was always a big support with her faith and encouragement.

### Did this experience change you? How?

Loren: Yes. The way I think about cancer and treatments available.

Sarah: Yes. It made me realize that it's important to enjoy the time we have together because we don't know how much time there will be.

Mom: Yes. I realize that life is short and it's important to take the time for a hug and to say "I love you"

### Did I change as a result of breast cancer diagnosis? How

Loren: You are far more supportive of women with breast cancer. You are more at ease with life.

Sarah: You've been a lot more health conscious.

Mom: You have always been a loving daughter and that didn't change at all. I believe that you are more serious about the plans and projects you create and find ways to complete them.

### Is there anything you would like to say TO breast cancer?

Loren: I wonder why there is so much. It can strain marriages and relationships.

Sarah: Yes. You Suck!

Mom: Yes. I believe that breast cancer (all cancer) comes from the pits of hell and that it is on its way back home to stay.

What do you thing about my tattoo?

Loren: I like the colors. That's all he was allowed to say.

"I know what I am doing. I have it all planned out,
plans to take care of you, not abandon you, plans to
give you the future you hope for. When you call on me,
when you come and pray to me, I'll listen.
When you come looking for me, you'll find me."

— *Jeremiah 29:11-13*

# Acknowledgements

There are so many people who helped me get this book written. I hope I don't leave anyone out. I need to first thank Beverly Vote. She has mentored me and held my hand all along this journey. She has encouraged me and given me the permission to be passionate about what I write. I want to thank the Writers Workshop gals who listened and gave feedback when I had concerns or ideas that I wasn't sure about. Thank you, Julene, for typing up the first rough draft. It was truly a labor of love. I want to thank my mom, Sarah, and Loren for being willing to complete that questionnaire. I know it wasn't easy. A special thank you goes to Joe Guse and Diana De la cerna. You were so generous with your information. I want to thank the ladies who gave me some funny stories to include in this book. Thank you: Kari, Wendy, Ramona, Julie, Heather, Mary Ann, Lakenia, Brenda, and Jill. I want to thank the dear ladies who read the book and critiqued it for me. Thank you: Tammy, Tina, Nicki, Connie A, Helen, Jeanna, Laura, Claudia and Gina for your support and kind words.

My greatest gratitude is to God. He put this book in my heart and kept reminding me that I had something that needed to be done. I was so blessed to be able to go to a Writer's Workshop and the book took on a life of its own. I hope you find this book a blessing and it makes your life more joyful and full of laughter.

# Endorsements

"As a breast cancer survivor and a Registered Nurse/Respiratory Therapist, Healing Laughter breathes truth into believing that training your brain into happiness and using positive thinking, along with laughter is a necessity, as well as the key to survival of cancer."

— *Tina Sue Perzee, RN, BSN, RRT*

"I felt like a little piece of every survivor is in this book! Connielee and her family let you know, in their own way, you as a warrior are not in this alone. Live, love, learn, cry, and most of all LAUGH!!"

— *Nicki Lloyd, Breast cancer survivor*

"As a cancer survivor myself, who had a similar experience to Connielee, I was thrilled to read this. Not only was it well researched, informative, and entertaining, it contains some really useful strategies to use if you or someone you know faces a cancer diagnosis.
Highly recommended."

— *Helen Williamson*

"Connielee got it right! Keeping one's sense of humor through cancer is so important; sharing her ability to find humor during treatment shows us that it can be done. Chin up, shoulders back, we can do it."

— *Tammy Bishop, two-time breast cancer survivor*

"Think of the beauty still left around you
and be happy."

— *Anne Frank*